ACKNOWLEDGEMENTS

Grateful acknowledgements are made to the following journals and anthologies where some of these texts appeared, sometimes under different titles and in slightly different form:

Asymptote, Atlanta Review, The Banyan Review, International Poetry Review, The Café Review, ērātiō, Four Centuries of Russian Poetry, Harpy Hybrid Review, Inventory, Little Star, On the Seawall, Plume, The Plume Anthology of Poetry, Transitions, Verseville, Unlikely Stories.

TRANSLATORS

"The End of the Myth", "Alexandra's Book. Sunset, Newark, NJ", "Ophelia", "In the Right-of-Way", "New Moon", "All that happened to me...", "Morning at Cape Cod", and "In Twilight. January 1st" translated by Boris Dralyuk.

"Ritual. Before Snow" translated by Maria Bloshteyn and Boris Dralyuk.

"Renga. 2020" was written in English.

All other titles, in verse and in prose, translated by Maria Bloshteyn.

TRANSLATORS' NOTE

It is an extraordinary experience for a translator to work with a poet who has such excellent command of the target language. Irina Mashinski writes verse and prose in Russian and English, and her sense of phrasing is equally exquisite in both tongues. In our experience, what began as translations of her Russian poems often grew into substantially reconceived original poems – results of collaborative authorship. Ideally, all translations ought to rise to that standard, but not all do. In this case, with Irina's help, we attained our ideal every time. It is a thrill to see the poems we love in Russian begin new lives in their new environment, and to know that we have played a part in this resettlement.

CONTENTS

Part 1. On the Other Side

Part 2. Military March

Part 3. In Absentia

Part 4. The Worm and the Cinder

Part 5. Texts

GIORNATA

Part 1. ON THE OTHER SIDE

The Black Eagle *(Aquila Verreauxii)* At Dawn

He falls asleep easily,
easily wakes –

at once regaining strength and
voice –
direct, without shades, evasions,
or an incline –
as if he hadn't been away –
cast in his own mould

He mounts – and scans the earthscapes below,
his arid realm,
to the nearest borders
of his self-chosen pale.
But "Africa" or, say,
his own name, or the one he carries on his
serrated wings
– Verreaux –
he neither knows nor needs.

He wakes at once,
nothing lost, spilled, or taken beyond his needs.

Thrust. A fan opening up –
like leaves of a giant tree
and within him
          – that span set on a vertical –
is all of you,
whole,
seen only in waking.

The Right-of-Way at Sunset (I)

A swath of public lands, forlorn, hemmed in,
sawn into denim double stitch by a ravine,
at either side a colonnade
(a smoking Vineyard,
a caustic Windyard)

the shrub glows gold over that rose ravine
another year awaits beyond the door, unseen,
and, like the sunrise, hot,
harsh sunset tarries not,
there's nothing left to hold.

A cleft was left after a peak rose higher,
but all that seared and burned is still afire,
from clouds down to the ground
ravine exists as one,
within it, life abounds –

from a pebble down below, to a birthmark on your brow,
from a pebble laid on grandma's new headstone,
to widow's black plateau,
afloat in golden glow
you pour to overflow.

For one who'd lost – a waste,
a no man's strand,
but the rushlight burns, it's steady till the end.
And on these unclaimed heights
I live our unlived life.

Where lands were reft, let gulleys stitch them fast.
Light's blinded outrider – last sunray hits the dust,
above the western range,
the day prolongs the change
clenching its last gold leaf.

But gold has finally set and platinum released,
and what was in the works – by dusk resolved with ease,
And look, a squirrel weaves
between smooth trunks – in flight
so needle-like, so light.

On the Other Side

I live on the other side of the Hudson,
where people don't live
(as one likeable man put it),
in a small town where there's no point
to owning a dress
and no particular weather

I'm one of those who sit
back to front
in the train car –
one cheek
to the racing
identical
tree trunks

Born late,
I live a latecomer
falling behind
all I liked
as we fell behind the West
in our Soviet youth

stumbling
just as our Speedola short-wave
was trying to fish out
Dire Straits
from the storm of the jammers –
but more often
the surrogate West –
Poland – would pop up,
rock and jazz
by their daring radio jockeys

– in the drawn-out twilight of morning
the dull gleam
of the plastic tabletop
in the kitchen with a window
out to a psychiatric ward
the radio's notched panel
with patterns of crumbs
streaked ivory patina
Baltic shallows
with amber bits
– can't dig them out with a knife –
the honey cake we ate together
back in the seventies

in that first – no, second – flat
in Zamoskvorechie
in Zamostie –
just two days ago
we'd awake having fallen behind
our near ones and the others
away from it all

The End of the Myth

Who's left? Maria, Serge
and Olya.
      Grandma and you.
As for the "voice of blood", its surge
        abated –
             So,

    what's left? Only unkindred voices
of places far away, unnamed –
        it flies, piercing the plexiglass of air,
    and finds me now –

a random soul – it hears
the weakest cry.
      Who's gone star-picking, with woven baskets
        of grapevine rays?

Alexandra's Book. Sunset in Newark

For grandmother

You're dozing off, waiting for me, all dressed up –
the table is laid and the door's unlocked:

right from the threshold I see that 100-watt
snow-white table cloth, and your Moscow teacups –

their skies like cobalt, and when I fill them
a gilded wave frills their afternoon brinks,

sails rise and fall in its ruffle as on a silk
folding screen. How I like how you talk, the rustle

of candy foil that you fold and unfold, time and again,
smooth with your nail – a narrow, fragile

bookmark in your tale, in the bold, fair dawn
of them all – Liza, Fanny, Zina, Shura, Lyonechka, Anna –

with music over that southern river, a search up in that Moscow flat
with my people's faces facing the bandit state.

Ivy Hill climbs through the window at sunset, flashes, then blinks off,
but the amalgam lingers between buildings, a folded strip of foil.

There, far away, one wave calms another,
this is not a full stop, this is only a comma.

Water calms water, wave consoles wave –
and what hasn't yet happened will have, will have.

Ritual. Before Snow

At the Jewish cemetery – no pebble to be found
all picked up and carried off
onto its chessboard grounds.

I search along
the edge of its grey lawn
and find an asphalt wedge
with an embedded stray
sliver –
can't pick it out, can't break it off –

I carry it with the forbidden flowers
to see you, as I had done in Newark –
for tea, and always staying late.

Outside, the day's as dark
as it had started, twinned by the window,
the headlights glow
as if wrapped in cellophane.
I'm driving home,
I'll wash my hands, get warm.

New Jersey earth's forlorn
about to break down
into black and white fields.

walking blues

cars leave the garages, back into the street
the men get into the driver seat
(but sometimes, it's the ladies)

stooping down, bending their knees
all and sundry, they wedge and squeeze
in
      – and slowly steer out of the garage

though unimpressive like the rest
this proudly sullen, small-town X
is still hard to leave, come morning.

I glance at the signs saying
STOP
— and walk right by, past the closed pawnshop,
with the "we buy gold" in the window

the morning rolls toward nightfall,
like an unrolling sutra scroll
as I walk to the station

this, one could say, is life in paradise,
so, we must be in heaven – d'you hear? a bird cries
in the red tree

Émigré*

One – a citizen of France
Romanian-born Germanic
Jew
squinting in the sunshine,
rewrote Yesenin
in what happened to be
German.

Another – half-German and half-Brit
from Vyborg –
taken across to Finland on a child's sled –
just in time, truth be told, before
all those Februaried Octobers
and snowstorms,
but didn't last in Finnish school,
where he was bullied,
this time as a Russian,
and was thrust into a
Swedish boarding school,
elite – as they'd say now.
So it was in Swedish that he began
to crudely build
up
sideways
as if with blocks
in alien's short lines –
and suddenly the sun emerged.

Poetry, train station galaxy!
Celan's entire sun

---

* P.Celan, H.Parland, B.Pasternak, G.M.Hopkins.

a single
undispersed
white frightening light.
And what about my Parland? Coursing
in the scarlet cabriolet
suddenly
at 22
(in boring Kaunas, exiled by his father)
lost to scarlet fever like a child.

Another yearned for music,
slitting the veins
of criss-crossed window frames,
neither Jew, nor convert
– and became a poet.

Another, an Anglican – turned Jesuit,
abandoned by his family,
and himself,
reached out to lines –
awkward
fragile
slate pencil, timid marks,
hikes with a friend along the hills of Wales – became a poet
and died in foreign,
coldly-passionate Dublin.
His poems
strange and premature,
hygienically burned
by his Jesuit brothers
and I, a stranger, weep for him.

Poetry. Great desert,
silk routes intersecting.

No point
in looking for your yesterself.
Your
prayer
language
gender
orbit
stayed the same –
then have you been alive?

Fall asleep one man
and awake another.

All burns the same
down in the kiln
bizarrely intermixed
go figure
where the kindling
comes from.

Stepping Out

For Mom

And what else is left? – pack up your haul,
put a pinch of ash in two or three palms,
stash whatever swept by in your eye,
take a coin for one ride.

And what else is left? – A wakeful light
hidden from the mind,
gliding, trailing,
so everything unsaid will stay unsaid.

With dark sense, dark milk in a jug,
I walk out onto the road:
daybreak, a river,
hardening loam.

At dawn, a range of mauve clouds
                              moves in.
Eyes shut, shutters shut.
Don't glower, cloud, that the light is out,
the west is cryptic, the east is dark.

Like meaning itself, twilight is dim.
The milk is darkening under the rim.
Who knows where the road flows,
who's leaving that house?

Part 2. MILITARY MARCH

Ode

You still laugh like a stranger about it:
we know not, yet go at it unfazed.
But my life is crumpling already –
carbon paper under your gaze.

They load us up at the station,
they shave our heads bald.
You look like a boy, *Homo stranger*,
you resemble no one at all.

That is just the beginning – some sketches,
blue vitriol on the sky's plaque,
but the wagons are coupling already,
and ruthlessly jumping the tracks.

I don't fear our pointless meeting,
nor the dull hashing out of our plot,
nor the post-breakup whining and bleating,
nor remembrance, nor all I forgot –

you will never be called for or dreamed of,
as the tracks glisten like blades.
I will only turn back for a moment,
at the skies painted with blood.

You gave me a glimpse of such freedom –
fleeting freedom – the very last frame.
You will never be called for or dreamed of –
I won't utter your second-hand name.

St. Petersburg Military March

And what we were left with
is the rutted
empire's
border decay
a grimly-imperial
order,
unwavering obdurate ways.

Smoke pillars
spiraling upwards,
decked cards
of courtyards laid low,
Kraft's old chocolate factory
crumbling to bits
on the snow.

Slag heaps lit up
by the streetlamps –
polished up
shame
shining hard,
the city snow packed, speckled,
but there's an arch to the yard.

This corner,
an old woman's elbow –
its anonymous bricks haven't thrived,
pissed on and spat on
and shattered,
yet the arch over them is alive.

Away from Ocean's Pull

My family name, waving her mermaid tail
tells me, admittedly, a different tale
than she would care admit.

But her fish scales flash cyan,
two vowels splitting at her fin
– which deep will echo back?

You reel her in but she just wriggles off,
no matter if you're Gilgamesh or Beowulf,
mere fisherman or Orpheus himself.

But move away from her and she will cleave,
a ray of light into a watery dark, she'll give
a nudge to his untouched rib.

Deep in the night, between the river banks,
past rusty anchors, chains with broken links,
without a splash, she'll show up at your door.

Coiling herself around the scaling beacon,
it's not the breeze that she is drinking –
her thirst's for something else.

She sees a hump rise black above the flow –
hears music pouring from it, hot and raw,
a husky voice is channeling Janis Joplin.

– Over a dark abyss that's shallow but our own,
that second-rate Titanic's trudging on
past a bell tower submerged mid-waterway.

But silliest ditties move the most when sung –
she listens till her heart is wrung,
then takes a breath and surfaces off starboard.

One touch, and then she swims beside the hull,
leading it upstream, far from ocean's pull
from the crude stare of oily *mortem.*

In nacreous dawn, not parting but apart,
riskily close to fireworks and sparks,
to rocking dancers, swaying decks, and lifeboats,

with riverweed that's wound round her wrist,
half-veiled by rising river mist
with locks of foam over her gleaming forehead –

swim on, swim on,
I'll be your guiding light.

Father. In the Hospital

November's face
faces itself
erased – it flows back down

back in the room,
unable to find his bed
an old hand recognizes
himself

only by turning away from himself
he recognizes himself

how he looked
through us
onto the mutely riotous woods
into the inside-out foliage
hiding the very last leaf

When a man dies...

When a man dies...

Anna Akhmatova

When a man dies, life with him begins anew
when a parent dies, life with him begins anew
breaking off along the notched edge,
the wedge breaking into a myriad word crumbs
a tiresome truth turns into a joke, an untruth,
now all his biases, all superstitions—
seem like a first endearment

In Twilight. January 1st

I'll get it – just a little more and ...
I'll stand on tiptoe in the morning,
and then, come evening, I will reach
the tender fir tree's ticklish withers,
forget about myself beneath it,
and feel the topmost needle's touch.

All morning, the accordion's
complaints sang out, the worrying
over my palm's unlengthy line.
But toward evening, you are higher
than yourself – look, from the spire:
the tree, the winding road, the moon.

As if you're on the downward slope of
your own years – so bright and hopeless,
alone, inside a rocking tram.
The view's the same – and yet it's altered.
Whom will you tell that you've just started,
a new force pulses through your palm?

On the Outskirts

The closer to the subway, the noisier and brighter,
the puddles grow wider and shallower,
      the streetlamps more pointless
Jupiter rotates swiftly and is hence everchanging,
Saturn, on the other hand, is so light,
give it water, it floats

Poetry fills up drums canisters garbage cans...

Poetry fills up drums canisters garbage cans
lakes bogs artificial reservoirs
ponds up ponds
landslides down slopes
dragging hamlets behind it
from the russet loins
of a volcano
splashes out onto a plateau

or else
a cart with its belly pressed into the ground
its wheels square
rolls
down
a damp forest's edge
gaining speed
here we go,
   here we go,
     it'll be a doozie
the tracks thaw in the sun, walls
shimmer with a tarnished silver *la poesie*

the word wants to fill itself
and yet it cannot
like a trick glass double-walled
all the way up its throat

The Right-of-Way at Sunset (II)

A barren wasteland lies
mid one-eyed Sunday huts
fierce Sunday sunset burns
the distant skies are dust
      My resurrected voice

A caustic right-of-way –
crushed blazing glass
between
two smoking towns
awakes
absorbs the tepid smoke

Tapestry

I slept – as if pursuing, or in flight –
my life, meanwhile, was grazing by my side,
not sparing me – thank God! – a single thought.
So I submerged and crossed the road.

Dusk came, rain merged with snow,
the trucks were muddying the scene,
thundering heavily, pressing into sleet.
And then I got my elbow free.

Behind my back, my life went streaming
so slowly-swiftly, as if I were weaving
a textured tapestry, featuring a creek,
a copse, a meadow, and a drunken shriek.

Angels – not lightning – flashed their wings
and slid into the clouds – I didn't finish weaving
the second sleeve, my knitting wasn't done –
and with that wing I swept up the horizon.

I outran life and leaned over the world's
edge – gazed at the cramped reverse,
the flip side, with its loops of thread.
How stunningly familiar it was.

Sky, Your Highness...

Sky, Your Highness,
Field, Your Majesty —
no need to get personal,
don't ask for ID.

Can't you just let me be?
Since when do you police?
I want to stay anonymous,
unfeeling, crumpled, creased.

Draped by the snow's white blanket,
a mere bump on the landscape,
just guessed at, featureless
beneath the mask:

a speck, a mere splinter
in a harvested field –
in a twilit photo,
a sharp jagged nick.

Let the grain be utterly featureless
in a place of exceptional flatness,
just a restless speck staring:
come lift me up.

Ophelia

She swam and sang...

I slept to you,
slept into you,
and then, to fall asleep, escaped from you
behind a cardboard wall, as if unbound,
alone.
I wove July with you – I wove and sang,
parting the silt like arras.
Just as you wanted, there was light,
there was my wanting what you wanted.
And sank, and sang, and swam.
You slept. Clouds lay above,
as if unbound, without sleep, without a blanket.

In the Right-of-Way[*]

However much the forest cuts the heart,
the forest is our home.
I've come back to the barren right-of-way
for us to stay.

With wolves, I will be numb and you don't howl,
be woods, be numb, learn how
to know like wolves, to drink like birds,
weave nests no more.

---

* Russian proverb: One who lives with wolves must howl like the wolves.

New Moon

For Stephan

Risen now,
molded of dull gold, bent and drawn
from a sheath,
as promised, on the left,
laid out on black calico.

Engulfed now,
as bequeathed,
by each ringing alpha and beta,
now laid bare,
scattered names in the dome.

"No one is needed" now
is irrelevant.
Here they move – waves behind
the resilient wall, churning, vaguely familiar,
on the left, against the breakwater,
but how arbitrary it sounds: "heart"!

Bent now,
life poured into a tight bottleneck –
but nothing is filled,
or budged even half-
way, or changed

with our arrival-departure –
as a heavenly creature,
light-heavy, with a brown or scarlet or
lackluster lining,
with such-and-such fate or habit.

What did it mean –
"trust in," say, or "don't trust in" –
when it beat against the breakwater all night,
against the opaque wall – but it bent,
didn't give, this wall
of the house with only one door?

All that happened to me...

All that happened to me,
happens not to be me.
Wait awhile, a dawn is in sight.
All around, like black ice –
gleaming – moonlit, amazed –
the bluest of blue anthracite.

Like an eyelash, the wind
gently curves in the night –
the felt of a bottomless sky.
Here's the very last mile –
now be brave, heading down
the last parsec's unraveling skew.

Here is the cobalt
of a hat's crumpled crown,
along with its wide, nappy brim.
A fine print lines its edge –
if the dipper should tilt,
it'll rain polar graupel and rime.

Part 3. IN ABSENTIA

In Absentia

Lento sostenuto

I. The Woodstove

To be alone takes skill,
especially at nightfall,
with a lit lamp and wine
to live the day out fully –
not letting it slip by,
not stooping
to a detective story,
and even if you stoop –
stop watching, reading
in midtrack,
come to
glance through that window
onto the frozen lake –
and rise

to check on the long-cold woodstove,
as if it were a child,
crouching beside it (rattling the door,
peeking inside, as he would do)
take out the
warped
still hot
ash pan –
it's full of sparks
and sticks, jutting out
of the overflowing ember Pompey –

and carefully, the ashes still alive,
stirring ever so slightly with each breath –
push first with the knee, then hip
the stubborn door
out to the porch
that lives a separate life
and to take out into the bone-breaking cold
the smouldering, shimmering, trembling,
smoking square
of ashes,

down snowy stairs,
both feet on each iced-over step
blindly
into the glazed moonlight,
while holding all that's left
down to the earth, the snowy ground,

but just a step short
of the brook
filled with fresh snow
lit up as if by a projector
lose grip
and spill it all
right by your slippered feet,
the scorching circle turning dark,
becoming earth and settling on the snowbank.

To be alone
and, lowering the ash pan
together with its hardened remnants
stuck in corners
and a single spark
to raise your empty level face –
reflected replica of January moon –
toward the racing, pine-filled
darkness crammed with light,
to stand there in the snow,

an equal to the lofty fir
to stand there as an equal,
replying to the stars –
lone soldier
in her forest foxhole.

II. January Again

Midnight stops in its tracks like a detached train car,
where you sleep now, my boy, it's all
ashes and cinder.

Wanderer, are you still called the same?
  — What was that nickname you had for me?
  — And that name
I had for you?

I dream your dreams now,
              junctions of empty platforms
but by 5 am – bang! – I fall into the colloidal chloroform
of summer – just look how your bush burns
– all you cared for, for what you cared returns.

The leaves of your bush, or tree,
fill my life like those words you wrote
in that Note, that last Note you wrote at 2:30 am,
then a new winter came,
then another. The ash won't go in the pail.
Everything turns July and melts – snow or hail.
I rattle the cast iron door as I stoke the stove,
it's with this stove I love, with all this ash I love.

Holding a copper scoop and a cast iron pail,
which one of us is walking away?
Who watches the golden smoke tower grow?
Who stands in the dark with your ashes aglow?

July-frost clearly sees through it all.
Who went out for a smoke – and the yard became small?

Who is these firs' equal, their spire-rays?
Whatever lies down will melt away.

Who went out for a smoke – and now wanders light,
a flake, a tattooed butterfly
as familiar to the lips
as your ash to the wave?

III. The Lake. Radiance

Inside the house it seems that darkness fell, but at the lake it's light,
                                    and the new moon is out.
The lake is glistening – dragonflies,
      tiny gliders skirr, nearly skimming the water.

A mist hangs over the contraction plane,
a halo, a glow of amniotic waters –
face down,
the surface now seems lifeless –
touch it – and it will tear
sending it all into the silt: July,
the axe-like house and the hacksaw forest.

Inside the house it seems it's nightfall, the lit lamp casts a crooked oval of light,
braiding through the wine bottles,
a cloistered cache of them.
Why do I store them still
beneath the hanging spiral staircase? –
the bottles clang when I climb up
into the bedroom
where I have already overwintered.
I walk up – in the cooled-off darkness
underneath me there is a gleam, as if in parting,
of malbec sentries,
shoulders rounded.
July, blood red, is fast approaching.

July approaches and that day is nearing.
A godless world in lakeside gloaming
is seen by God down to its bottom.
When autumn comes, I know, the shroud will fall,
slip off, pollen and algae –
the lake that lies deep in the mountain paws
will shrink by autumn,
the water of the bared lake will turn
lightweight and empty
and in August
I'll swim across it to the other side.

IV. In the Water

Across a sunset lake
into the cooled off east
I'm swimming, gliding light,
toward the mountain rim,

as if I'm drawn along,
my head aloft and dry –
the ridge's crookback woods
plunge deep into the sky

their strand of jagged tops,
(a dent but not a gash)
as if I could traverse
the skybrow's scarred flesh,

Tectonic oar-sprung ridge
turns darker than a plum
(...there, tangled on my left,
 lies a small isle Absalom...)

– I'm borne upon three whales
through waters clear and free.
Then, carried from the shore:
"Look, Mommy, d'you see?

Look! What's that animal?!"
The child is right, of course.
I swim with you inside,
through stems of watergrass,

the copper sunset sinks –
a coin handful, tossed,
each lingering moment spent
is lost.

It's almost gone... no, wait.
The long day's final action:
a cloud glows all alone
above a cobalt boat's reflection.

The surface empties. Swarming midges
glow on the other shore
– another one awaits you there
transforming you once more.

V. Forest Fire

Last night the woods were burning –
today they're not.
I'll step out on our deck. That morning –
remember our first breakfast here?
    — we dragged our wobbly chairs outside,
as if we had stockpiled
woodland days
for happiness and work.

Now shut that window over the kitchen sink –
the sunset lies in ambush
it's burning through the dust.
Out there it's all woods, never orchard.
Out there – the woods, the thicket,
all that's lost,
tree litter, leaf debris,
half-eaten scraps, stumps, shed skins,
horsetail and mosses,
a stillness of ferns,
and chipmunks, those forest racers,
the messengers of woodland CNN.

Last night, Prince was the news,
today as well.
He was your age, no, slightly
younger,
but last night he caught up.
Why did he die? –
they carry on at CNN.
Squinting at the sun,

I load the dishes in the sink,
there's no peace,
but leaves can sleep.

Just look at how I steer along,
how calmly I walk into the Room.
But last night's smoke
seeps in and settles in the throat,
reminds of you once more,
as does all water.

How our lake glitters at 6 am,
how ruthless are the afternoons.
Pierced by the sunset, slowly, brightly,
the fearsome house turns heavy –
leave it, run –
I drive out to the landfill.
Here the road splits –
once, we almost got that house –
the blue one, way up on the cliff,
and we'd be living there,
July would come and go
but you'd remain –
would these woods still burn?

VI. Twilight 1

The tree is dead,
I drag it down the slope,
half-sinking in the snowbanks.

So will my Faustian questers
someday
haul me through the snow,
in just such tin-stiff mittens,
all my odd loops and whorls,
this tangle, knots upon the bark –
a pattern seen but once.

And just as quiet and pale
as these stunned trees,
my brother-poets will
escort me:
the icy beech, the hemlock, the black walnut,
the birch, the hornbeam, the bird cherry,
the sugar maple, the plantain, the other maple –
that for a long time will burn
scarlet.

When I'll be dragged
blinded over the stumps –
through the gully,
over remnants of fencing,
the forked road, the post,
the plaster fountain –
the birdbath overturned,
the empty birdhouse, rot and moss,
the gulley, and the rot and moss,

when I'll be dragged
down for the extraction
of the golden root –

a ragged trench will stretch across the deep snow,
stippled like a greyhound,
as if the angels wrestled on it,

they'll stand there scattered in farewell,
the slope as deep as a fresh rough-draft,
not noticing how their legs are whipped
awkwardly by my dead branches,
by the trailing
still unyielding roots.

VII. Staying Put

Glancing through the small streaked window
at the gleaming Dalmatian slope,
I wash a dish or two
in the sink with its chipped corner –
the only source of light in March
inside the house
with a shaky winding staircase,
a house that never scaled that slope
and has gone cold without him,
a plywood house
cobbled together
back in the seventies
by an artless settler,
avid collector
of *The Geographic*

VIII. At Dawn

A squirrel rustles in stiff russet leaves,
a housewife rummaging
through her empty household
– a house hole,
with a hollow at the heart
How odd and brittle the words
how dull and how finite:
household, dish load, depot
left after a life lived – but again
tons of cast iron
turns pliable tin,
pulpy *is* emerges from the hard been
together again, animal and implement
rummage in that rusty abject courageous
pile of a life,
its shed leaves
The sackcloth thins out,
torn by stars

How quickly the light gets through
    warms up
        and,
            for the umpteenth time
                comes the fast train
                    of dawn
                        the color of rails

All the same, all the same:
go on with Your housekeeping,
wounding and cutting –
the reel keeps on rolling
You just can't get enough

IX. Coming Home

The one who died isn't flying home
                              with me
he'll return first on his own
meeting me there as if nothing happened,
overjoyed as I open the windows
It's only on route that he is by my side
losing then finding his glasses
getting lost in
unfamiliar coin
stumbling on construction site planks
too narrow for two
marveling at all in sight
listening in to the new vernacular
as if he isn't from around here
perching on my shoulder and sharing
all my ridiculous
meetings and missings
He's there with me at the last
trolleybus stop
wandering and breathing in
old familiar slippers-and-cabbage smell of Moscow
stairwells
standing patiently
not rushing me on
in front of the scuffed matted door
of those I wanted you to meet
who waited in vain and are gone

X. The First Spring

First thing, I open all the windows.
Then it's off to get the mail. Down by the hill's foot
I turn onto a crooked road – it opens
up into a familiar light.

Out there an apple tree still darkens where the road parts
– last month, an ice rink lay below.
Two local ducks,
and one child
would take up an entire leafless limb.
A mere stump, and not an apple tree.

Then suddenly, I once again remember
the death of our small family.
Away from everyone I gather
my fallen apples scattered by the tree.

XI. At Twilight 2

Today I'm Mrs. – not Mr. – Nabokov
standing here in the yard in my red
faded boots
and my stepson's oversized plaid shirt
I assembled the leaf blower myself and I stand
breaking apart last year's matted foliage
watching indifferently
as the weighty top rotted layer
lifts and I steer
these heavy tsunami
one after the other
into the ravine by the shed

It's the time when
dreams fill
with my dead, mountains
block what's left of the sun

They darken toward evening,
first one, then the second, the third,
they linger, turning mauve, and move off to the west,
like leaves to the ravine

XII. Still-life with a Sink, a Glass Shelf and a Window

The day is bright, though sunless
— just peek into the bathroom—
isn't it fine, this cut-glass light?

The deck of blades slides
   face-first into the glass shelf –
        the sparkling tongue

of a glacier, an avalanche.

            But here, right in the corner,
so near
down in that burrow behind the mirror
in the gloaming over the sink's abyss —
seven years gone unnoticed,
their wooden dull horizon.

Here, in the back, there is a bottle,
almost full –
the blue
        Gillette (to open
cautiously, smell, close the cap),
                        here

lies the toothpaste tube, neck twisted,
        as if it's leaning for a chat down from a berth bed,
its dried-out, buckling
        choking collar

– but where's that screw-on cap
  rolling so nimbly
          under the toilet tank?

XIII. Rain on Route 15

The drivers act like kids
spotting a police car
they slow down hastily
and crane their rubber necks,

and flock together, bunch before the toll booth,
then line up in a queue, all single file,
and how obedient, goodness, how sad
for every x in the equation

[the wet Ford police cruiser
sits ducklike on the grassy median strip
and faces east
in wait for his next victim]

The second twilight gathers
                      and the anthems
of cars join in a single Hallelujah

[obsessive search for snake-proof boots
for me, not sparing –
we thought money, but it turned out – days,

burst into a just-closed store
and shouted – I was embarrassed]

— Okay, we all line up –
now comes the crush
right by the entrance

[how smooth
the officer's cheeks, how cold, how calm...]

And in each
            and every one
                    the wipers swish –
you hear – the rain
        you hear – it's Leonard Cohen!

The road keeps rising steadily
slicing off one dark hill after the next
like heads
now comes the free-for-all

[he can't care less, he isn't sad
for anyone, he doesn't know the story
and how we draw wicked
doodles on yellow post-it notes]

By the time I get there, it'll be night

A scarlet swell – what's that? –
the brake light spheres
– and suddenly I love you so again –

you are – I am – complete once more
it gets too warm –
now to get of my jacket

left cheek to anything that's sudden
– from a rolled-down window – a cigarette stub flying in reverse –
a crane
who lagged behind death on his flight
due North

Part 4. THE WORM AND THE CINDER

The Jordan River

Up to my shins in muddy Jordan, yellow like Yangtse
I'm standing at the border, at the boundary.

The crowds pour into the souvenir stall,
the river flows south in a loamy sprawl.

Pilgrims from a country that's no more,
in dripping "I [heart] Jordan" t-shirts sing on the shore.

I see you in the reeds, smoking your pipe, eyeing the scene –
how righteously Russian, how keenly they sing! –

glancing at the pilgrim busses, their melting rubber,
or down at a stem where a mendicant spider

crawls home, like in Uglich, and the skies' coal smolders
just like night coals glow on your milk-white shoulder

in the backwoods, our roof soaked by the rain
on those easy days when you're alive again.

Then you look back laughing – a lightening bolt,
and, a pillar of loamy tears, I say, stop.

Renga. 2020

Let it cut more deeply.

Hafiz

In the cold spring, cut deeply into this hill by the lake,
I crouch in front of the cast iron wood stove, just like he did
in the seven free months he had here.
Now it's me and the fire,
     and the action unfolding in flames.

The Worm and the Cinder

1.

Life is what fits within the worm
right now
and its length is the length of the worm
right now,

everything that pushes within him toward the exit
in the dusk on the jagged
edge between asphalt and earth, grass –
contracting, expanding into a long j,
while he is crawling together with the consumed,
the gravel and glass
scratch
his delicate esophagus,
    not allowing
the swallowed to clump
into a single grain.

Sharp pebbles, all the primaeval gravel
of the happened
stirring the insides,
the ashes,
igniting then letting
cool down again and again,

– behind him stretches
a scarlet streamlet, steaming,
rhythmically thickening,
branching out in veins,
dragging within him, and then after him
in the loam,

dredged in fine pale dust,
like a stretched-out grocery bag –
heaviness itself
stretched.

Trailing above him
the small scurf flakes
fanning out from a jet,
below –
trail, red in the ash.

Pain is unknown to him –
he would still crawl, had he known
its signals.
Cut him, hack him in two,
– he will still live the half as a whole,
aware of his former length.

The future enters his mouth
with the grass, humus,
bits of thin torn roots,
alfalfa clumps

and there
passes through the rings of his hearts
                    – *there my heart turned to wax,*
melted within my innards –
everything, everything through the wriggling worm
entering in, exiting out,
without being digested, as it was, as it is,
consumed chaos

remains: the exterior substance
chopped by his groundgrinder –
the past,
discarded
mince.

Minimalist,
he extracts
only that which he eats.

He doesn't have moods, only
that which enters his eyes,
he breathes with his skin, as is natural for him,
and pours out like water
on the pale trail
of the cooling-off loam.

A worm has eyes.
Deep in the dusk,
practically in the dark,
at the right of the turn,
on the slope
over the road –
stands a house with a burning-cinder window

severs the now from the now
on the curve
of the path
brighter toward nightfall,
where the jagged, pinesap-edged
cooling-down asphalt ended.

2.

Returning in the twilight,
practically in the dark,
up the roadside, along the left edge
between the asphalt and old grass,
and then suddenly at the curve,
on the hill on the right –
a house
the lit window
amid the dark trees,
smouldering, almost crumbling
into the barely lit yard –
a cinder –
scarlet with warm pale ash –
the innards of a house
where the worm is fed
moist newspapers
a wet mix
of important local news.

Then, beneath her jacket
suddenly shudders
that darkest, that dampest of days,

and above it
crawling back
compressing and expanding
the arch
        of primordial trees,
        a bag of leaves walks
its birthed chaos,

the flint
of twilight
scratched
by sharp quills.

The Worm and the Box

Suddenly at the curve,
on the slope –
with its lit
window
among the dark trees –
a cinder,
scarlet with pale ash –
smouldering, almost crumbling
into the barely lit yard,
the innards of a house
where the worm is fed
moist newspapers
a wet mix
of important local news.

Coming down the hill, she returns to her own home,
where the newspapers are dry,
she crams them into the cast-iron woodstove, and for the ump-
teenth
time takes out the full ash pan
with the jutting out unconsumed sticks
        the stems and leaves that have already
            turned peridot

  to that
completely empty
parking lot
of the darkening town, its only traffic light stuck on green –
from the long one-storey building that looks
like a closed empty shoe box,
carefully carries to the car, parked right at the edge,
                beside the messy border of the living grass,

a cardboard box,
that was handed over to her
in a purple recycled bag with their logo,
afraid to drop
the heavy human ashes

A Trace

Tout l'automne à la fin n'est plus qu'une tisane froide.

Francis Ponge

1.

A trace
on the giant empty parking lot of a mall
closed on Sundays.
A ruptured outline of a petrol lake-ink spot –
violet, apricot
on the asphalt coarse-grained signet,
overflow,
memory's ebb and flow – a trace
of the hot rhythmic object, its belly,
its jointed axels –
a stain in flux.

Memory, its muck enters the pitted asphalt
spends itself, melts

the trail,
all its hopeless joy.

2.

A trace,
oozes out of a thing's narrow bottleneck, loses
its form, stopped by the friction
of knowing
spends all of itself, shrinks along the edges.

That's how the outline ruptures,
losing the apricot smell of its rainbow
crumpled memory.

The gaze
left by a thing,
dissolves itself in the ground, plaiting the grass –
ofwhateverkind,
and the grass pushes through it,
the grass covers, transmutes it,
conceals
the trace of a thing, its makeup, its form,

a thing
spends, spills itself fully,
falling behind.

Geomorphology of a Hole

Grief wrenched out
by the roots
left behind a hollow,
a paleohole,
a void,

a passing ant slides down its slope
a passing downpour soaks the humus
and sprouts at once
with the still cryptic roots
their tangle –
mosses, then grass.

That's how life begins –
gains a foothold on this cavity-planet
covers the slope
as if with real greenness.

The ashen soil crumbles, turns to dust –
and just as it appears
a strong wind blows the ashlike continent away.

But for a long time yet, the roots
and the stout fresh stems of the half-empty
stalks,
their hollow fifes
hold back the shape.

That's how the hole matures
fiercely
moss pleurae
toil, pumping oxygen –
they can't not pump,

and moss darkens, first by blotches, then by steps,
a semblance of time,
uneven emerald
and jade –

the mosses and the lichens lighter than wormwood,
drenched by moonlight
(Rousseau!)
they must continue being.

Following them
come grasses –
sage and sedge –
untidy happiness here and there
in clumps and tufts,
march in, with their samurai hairdos,
and firmly hold on to
the cooled off
        crumbling slope.

Then a moon ray
seeks out the crater – it turns white with grass,
    reflecting the reflection.

Morning at Cape Cod

Toward the wave and back,
amid the flock, behind it –
    dear little sandpiper,
    my darling shorebird.

I'll walk along the sand,
I'll walk along the sandbar,
    toward the far-off dark –
    then reach it – and turn back.

No bridge, no pier, no dock –
abutments in the distance,
    like people in a queue,
    stare at unseen vistas.

Their evenly spaced chain
keeps not a thing at bay.
    Around their rotten legs,
    waves follow other waves.

The world is turquoise-white –
blessed is she who sees
    the limpid net of waves,
    the rot of firm wet beams,

who walks right up to them –
to those familiar wrecks –
    and gently puts her palm
    atop their sultry necks,

who sees how strong they are,
emerging from the waves,
    both on their rotten sides
    and on their sultry sides.

With you – away from you,
with you – and after you,
    along the gleaming line,
    amid the sandpipers,

trapped in the past, brand new,
mindful and not at all,
    within myself, without.
    A swim – and I am whole.

The Morning of the Day when Mom Died

When I sleep in the car-womb near morning,
the whole world crowds in around me
lengthwise
the garbage trucks drive in
crosswise
the garbage trucks wedge in
  and leave, taking time to upend their trash cans
folding in half at the back, knees and
elbows jut out

nothing is strange to me
a wet rug is woven beside my head, it is all
– suspension, air, free reign
right by my head

between me
and all this birdlike, branchlike there is no
membrane
as if this is my only daybreak
my mottled brain became level and bare
the wet from the half-open window
is falling right into my hair

This Time Around

How awkwardly the leaf crosses the road
Brake!! ...
no!
thank goodness, just an uprooted stump –
not a moose
not a groundhog this time, not a raccoon
Not a deer
but a matress and bag
last year's leaf, and not a warm studded
hedgehog

Time after time this lump
on highway shoulders –
approaching –
the giant ripped-apart carcasses
on the edge
of your unscathed lane,
till you get a good look:
a tire!

exploded! and again
no –
probably for a straight half-a-mile
a massacre of tires
the likes of which hasn't been seen
At least one has been spared

If it only could always be thus –
the lichens take over a hill,
so it's not just the glacier-piled
boulders and pebbles
that gleam
with a light never seen

and there's no running out of
porcupines, turtles, and
    people

Giornata

A view of clouds through the window at sunset

A sky that's swinging open at both ends,
a cloud as indisputable as Rome,
set in a crooked frame of peeling white,
encasing mica, shimmering in the light,
beyond which float Colonna, colonnade,
the sunset's glow upon a vast façade,
a scarlet range, a staircase into Hades –
Last Judgement's awesome nimbostratus.

Above you glide cathedral and piazza,
a blazing fire that won't warm you,
sudden blinding flashes – paparazzi,
steepening clouds and streaming rays,
hunkering masters' backs, steep vertebrae,
and on their shoulders silver overlays
dull with patina, then coppices and chains,
whipped on by lean lashes of sanguine,

mighty shoulders twisted into spirals.
The least cloud's ablaze with its own candles,
while tip-toeing through the cordons,
all apprentices take flight
workshops of them flocking to the light.
But the work-worn hands of thunderclouds
still glow warm from daily toil,
weary nomads, slowly they repose.

I am standing here, my palms wide open,
vagabond fingers spread against the pane,
rings slide downward from the knuckles.
You are born a master only once.
Life flies onward, laughing, dry flakes falling –
paintwork on the sun-warmed frame is sloughing,
while the plaster of the day's prepped fresco
takes on the celestial forest grove.

I am standing here without the lights on,
while each branch is busy with its own song.
There's a mark high in the sky above my window,
the windowsill is, like a workbench, wide.
Laze the day away and it will end with this:
forests of scaffolding intact, spanning sky
end to end, as the celestial workshop leaves you –
see it float eastward, ever farther east.

Part 5. TEXTS

The Poet and the Child

Anyone who remembers, a lifetime ago, trying to make out new patterns on the wallpaper each night and being scared by the folds of that strange shape on the chair will understand what I am about to say. A poetic sensibility or sense – whether sixth or seventh – appears early in life; all children have it to a greater or lesser degree – a passion for likeness. To a child, the world appears to be a big house full of things and she, more than anyone, can sense their familial resemblances. This is not a metaphor, it is a morphogenetic law of life itself, which we discover in our childhood.

This is why children know the world so well. Strange-sounding substitutions in a child's speech seem entertaining and accidental only to grownups, who perceive things as existing independently of each other. The world of a grownup is dismembered and compartmentalized. It is rare that a grownup acts by association in everyday life – as rare as a slip of the tongue. How often do we shove a rake into the cuttlery drawer? For a child, however, a rake and a fork are, basically, one and the same. A child doesn't deal in labels but in the substance of things. Such deep metonymy requires unconditional faith. And it is faith that breaks down first. This is precisely what happens in adolescence.

Adolescents are antipoets. Hearing a metaphor, they raise their eyebrows: what are you babbling about? Try telling an adolescent a joke that hinges on metonymy. Try to explain an abstraction by a metaphor. It is only in youth that the original sense returns – but not to everyone. This is why there are millions of grownup adolescents living on this planet.

Poets are people who manage to keep alive what they discover in childhood (or who never manage to forget it): the law of universality. This is why it seems that poets know something about the future. To a child, a signifier is more than just a signifier. A child has trouble understanding what "just a symbol" means. For a child even a signifier is a thing unto itself. Actually, that's how children are taught: look, this letter looks just like a bagel, this one, like a slide. A poet is someone who gets stuck at this stage of mastering symbols.

A reader's love for poems is, among other things, a longing for a time when things were still things and not concepts. Once you get past your own internal barriers and all the screens and obstacles erected by the lyric poet, so that the path feels both virgin and memorable, you return to your own beginnings, when during the dreaded naptime an outlined rainbowy dot with a wiggly little tail would swim diagonally under your lowered eyelids, leaving a narrow disappearing trail – to when the world was mobile and shimmering with kinship.

And so, to this day, checkers long to be played by *Czechs* and *Czechs* hurry at *checkout*. And *broderie anglaise*, never actually handled and only read about, gives you the shivers, not because of what it and its cutwork look like, but because it makes you think of an inflamed throat or a spoonful of ice cream – when they cut out your tonsils, brought you home, and sat you down on the windowsill, on its *glazed* white expanse, before a winter windowpane frosted over with lacy swirls. A word is a smooth pebble in your mouth. Names are things.

The seeming chaos of poetic speech is simply a special way of putting the world into order, of battling chaos independently of, but parallel to, the logical route. This is why the poetic world, which lacks consistent correlations and is not regulated by the direct logic of concepts – this world of objectified meanings and all-permeating kinship – is off limits to those who've become irreversibly grownup, who have travelled too far upon the road at the beginning of which stands the symbol.

Behind the Wall

The mountain was looming there for a long time, waiting (for some reason, it always seemed to be in the East, to the right). What's more, everyone kept harping on it: Berlin! Berlin! I believed them all. Still, a trip wasn't happening – always either one thing or another.

I cautiously circled around it – not as a country or a land, but as an idea.

But every year the same images repeated of that day when the Wall fell, and for the countless time I'd decide – the already familiar faces, bodies, that crowd surging upward and over the top – this is it! Now, I'm going!

After all, I had to take Germany, so I did.

I didn't take the mountain though, but a motley hill, an expanse of pale brown rocks, yet another view from the train. The crumpled ticket I obediently hold in my hand – by the time you get to your stop, it sprouts little piles.

A diffused de-focus. The swirls, not on the glass looking out, but right there, outside, on the grass beyond, on the foliage beyond, on the forest and on the grove – tableaus at midday, a patchy shimmer, like in Nibelungen and Nosferatu. And even that bright and transparently pale sky looks not like a sky, but rather the fact of a sky. As if it is concealing something. Or trying to hide itself.

The landscape toward the South, to the Alps, looked like the word itself: *landscape* – as it spread out on the sod-covered folds of youngish but already worn mountains. On top of a well-trodden viewing deck I kept spinning round and round like a weathervane gone mad, to the amusement of my new acquaintances, as I was trying to superimpose a mental map (more real for me) onto reality (real for them): is that Italy over there? And that misty something – is it really Switzerland? Then we descended, chatting, and there it was again, my original destination, together with lupines, dusty railroad track grass, train platforms, their names, the sound of the language, which turned out to be not frightening at all, with its soft sod-like everyday tone, like the white cups in that café on a leisurely Saturday morning – across the road – see, it's just *Europe*, so what were you afraid of?

With its broken-up little cloud, with its hesitant sun reflecting off the still-wet scales of a university town, where I, of course, was searching for my brother-poet, and in another town, where I was looking for a different brother. With its stairs and staircases, with its multitudes of people sitting on these steps, mottled with man splotches, bird splotches. With the strangely familiar-looking dogs on the riverside embankment, where the twilight still lingered. With its slow, rippling river.

L. wrote me from Berlin: a law student is extolling the greatness of Deutschland on YouTube, and another one – not some skinhead, but another law student – is gently inviting sixteen-year-olds to join the cause. Another two-three percent – and they'll win in Brandenburg and in Thüringen.

And toward nightfall, the sky looks like Köln lager, as the light continues to linger above the riverside wharf with its hotshot-bicyclists – and I am sitting by myself at a long wooden table painted blue. Or else, leaning over the railing and looking at the riverboats, and the steamboats festooned with flags on a long northern night.

In Germany I slept like the dead, straight through.

And the cathedral. Well, of course, there was the cathedral. The columns inside – rootless trunks – were bathed in a lemony light at 7 in the morning. The rough-textured expanse of the flagstones, a bucket, a mop, and spilled soap.

In the lemony-black cathedral (right by the entrance, not choosing any particular spot), I placed a candle. Just one. It didn't start burning right away – I held it to another one (in memory of a him or a her), but then it did and was standing there burning by itself – a little bit off to the side. Then I returned and moved it, so that you wouldn't be alone – and suddenly I understood that I'm doing this for the last time. That even though you are not alive, you aren't dead, but just are. And we don't need this anymore.

Going off to America

Dear friend – well, yes, of course, that possibility always remains: to go off to America (if only you're not there to begin with). When even the Symphonie Fantastique sounds predictable – then, maybe, yes, the time has come. Then you can hang down, head first, press your ribcage painfully against the metal ribs of the bedframe, lean against the mattressed matrix of the elevator, peer into the elevator shaft in that far – faaar – away entrance, which smells of the shoe cabinet and someone else's cooking, and to guess at the hammock sagging into the netherworld below, that's right, to guess rather than see – all of it, to the overturned concave horizon, the unfamiliar underside of the world, with its excruciatingly embossed rhomboid plexus, all the sea stripes, interlaced with *terra incognita* or *tabulae rasae*, and black birds with their uneven jagged edges, hollering in the language that you've yet to learn – and only then can you cautiously touch the stiff satin dome, punctured by the pattern of beaks and knots. You won't believe how quickly things will start to happen then, how nimbly the glinting sun will twist and turn to face you, like a polished coin's heads, balancing on its ribbed edge, and the next moment the sailors are already peering mistrustfully into your documents, as if they're looking out at some finely-enameled horizon, and then the timeworn propeller winds up, and the movie projector begins to whir, and then the phantom, called *city M*, disappears in the foam of salty snow whipped up by the trolleybuses.

Of course, it's entirely possible to revive in Amortica, to begin anew and never be reborn. What you are asking about, what you are calling A-merica is neither this, nor that, nor the other, but a trying of the otherness, which is a *priori* impossible. Believe me, the negating *A* in "America" is not accidental – it's that ironic little taglet, a tag that chases you right into the heart of the nonexistent. Should you also try all that happened to me and to others like me – with my family, dragged to the other side, with a guitar made in a small Russian town with blue shutters and abnormally large apples, and, most vitally, with a carefully culled load of dusty vinyl records, oh, yes, and with another possession: a portable Yugoslavian typewriter, with its now forsaken Cyrillic and broken memories? You're thinking that to go off to America means to return all the cards to the dealer and to take new ones from the deck that contains everything, as we know, except cabbages and kings, including a river that flows through its improbable south and contains more s's than any other word. That's why (as you heard) the poet gave its name to the cat – the poet is dead, but Morton Street is there, with a symmetrical No.44 at its bended elbow – and there you are, starting from scratch.

It's only when you stand on some street corner on a brightly cold and barren October, only then will you learn that nothing in this world could ever be as lonely as that fall, dry firing a sweep of its cerulean blue leaves across the crumbling ochre sky. Yes, dear friend, this is it, the City, the one and only, which everyone knows inside out, and here are its percussion and horns, and here's its chimney stack – the City that's sitting all by its lonesome like some enormous Otis Company elevator, where everything only references itself, the cast iron heads and tails, the fences and cellars, and in the midst of the streets, right under the feet of the pedestrians, the stairways lead down to the gaping netherworld of the taverns with their warming smells of unfamiliar foods. And believe it or not, you forget quite easily that way over yonder – downward and all the way through to the other side – the early frost has come, and maybe, just maybe, the first light snow has freshly fallen.

So, let's say it began with a vinyl record gleaming through its thin, worn Soviet record sleeve, frost on that fallow field – the 2nd Concerto that an American needle never ended up touching. And now there are hollow Zen chimes clanging in the wind on a porch in the puritanical suburb across the river, a porch with the entrance door still bare of the Christmas wreath or breath. But I'll tell you one thing: someone who was happy back there, on those black – long before the coming of winter – vinyl fields with their wavy grooves, is happy here, in this antiworld, and doesn't notice that she's walking upside down. She is ready for anything, except the word "forever," and stands on the shore of the bird-covered bay, at the very edge of Unmerica, wrapped in a scarf as grainy as the earth itself, with the hardened scales of local foliage caught in its loops; she stands in this immobile, impossible, other life, while her smiling transparent double removes her salt-stained boots in the foyer.

ABOUT THE AUTHOR

Irina Mashinski was born and raised in Moscow. She graduated from Moscow University, where she studied theory of landscape and completed her PhD in paleoclimatology. In 1991, she emigrated to the United States, where she taught high school mathematics as well as literature, history, and meteorology at several universities. Mashinski is the author *The Naked World* (MadHat Press, 2022) and of eleven books of poetry and essays in Russian. She is co-editor, with Robert Chandler and Boris Dralyuk, of *The Penguin Book of Russian Poetry* (Penguin Classics, 2015) and of *Cardinal Points*, the journal of Brown University's Slavic Department. Her work has been translated into several languages and has appeared in numerous journals and anthologies both in the US and internationally.

Website: www.irinamashinski.com

ABOUT THE TRANSLATORS

Maria Bloshteyn's main scholarly interests lie in the field of literary and cultural exchange between Russia and the United States. She is the author of *The Making of a Counter-Culture Icon: Henry Miller's Dostoevsky* (University of Toronto Press, 2007), the translator of *Alexander Galich's Dress Rehearsal: A Story in Four Acts and Five Chapters* (Slavica, 2009) and Anton Chekhov's *The Prank* (NYRB Classics, 2015), and the editor of *Russia is Burning: Poems of the Great Patriotic War* (Smokestack Books, 2020). Her translations have appeared in a number of journals and anthologies, including *The Penguin Book of Russian Poetry* (Penguin Classics, 2015).

Boris Dralyuk is a poet and translator. He is the author of *My Hollywood and Other Poems*, co-editor (with Robert Chandler and Irina Mashinski) of *The Penguin Book of Russian Poetry*, editor of *1917: Stories and Poems from the Russian Revolution* and *Ten Poems from Russia*, and translator of books by Isaac Babel, Andrey Kurkov, Maxim Osipov, Leo Tolstoy, Mikhail Zoshchenko, and other authors. His poems have appeared in *The New York Review of Books, The Hopkins Review, The Hudson Review, The New Criterion*, and elsewhere, and his criticism and translations have appeared in the *Times Literary Supplement, the London Review of Books, Granta, The New Yorker*, among other venues.